AI and the Future of Advertising
Precise Targeting and Real-Time Analytics

Table of Contents

1. Introduction 1
2. The Rise of AI in Advertising 2
   - 2.1. The Advent of AI in Advertising 2
   - 2.2. From Traditional Advertising to AI-Infused Strategies 2
   - 2.3. Harnessing Machine Learning for Predictive Analysis 3
   - 2.4. AI and Programmatic Advertising 3
   - 2.5. The Future Of AI In Advertising 4
3. Understanding the Logic of AI and Machine Learning 5
   - 3.1. Artificial Intelligence: A Primer 5
   - 3.2. The Era of Machine Learning 5
   - 3.3. Supervised versus Unsupervised Learning Models 6
   - 3.4. Making Machines Learn: An Overview of ML Process 6
4. Unlocking the Potential of Precise Targeting 8
   - 4.1. Defining Precise Targeting 8
   - 4.2. The Role of AI in Precise Targeting 8
   - 4.3. Real-World Applications 9
   - 4.4. Harnessing the Right Data 10
   - 4.5. Leaps and Bounds: The Future of Precise Targeting 10
5. Exploring Real-Time Analytics and its Impact 12
   - 5.1. Understanding Real-Time Analytics 12
   - 5.2. The Intersection of AI and Real-time Analytics 13
   - 5.3. Impact of Real-Time Analytics on Advertising 13
   - 5.4. Challenges in Implementation 14
6. Cracking the Code: How Algorithms Shape Ads 16
   - 6.1. The Basics of Algorithms 16
   - 6.2. Advanced Algorithmic Techniques 17
   - 6.3. Real-life Applications of Algorithms 17
   - 6.4. Algorithms as Agents of Precision 18

- 6.5. The Future of Advertising Algorithms 18
- 7. Personalization and Predictive Analysis: The Future 20
  - 7.1. Role of AI in Personalization 20
  - 7.2. Importance of Predictive Analysis 21
  - 7.3. Combining Personalization with Predictive Analysis 21
  - 7.4. Real-Life Applications and Case Studies 22
  - 7.5. The Road Ahead: Challenges and Opportunities 23
- 8. The Ethical Considerations in AI Advertising 24
  - 8.1. Privacy Concerns 24
  - 8.2. Algorithmic Bias and Discrimination 25
  - 8.3. Transparency and Explainability 26
  - 8.4. The Monopoly Problem 26
- 9. Interpreting Big Data in Ads and Marketing 28
  - 9.1. The Role of Big Data in Advertising 28
  - 9.2. Big Data Analytics: Transforming Raw Data into Insights 29
  - 9.3. Real-time Analytics: Enabling Dynamic Marketing Strategies 30
- 10. Case Studies: Successes and Failures in AI Advertising 32
  - 10.1. The Netflix Algorithm: A Growth Engine 32
  - 10.2. Unilever: Improving Efficiency and Accuracy 33
  - 10.3. The Google Flu Trends Flop 33
  - 10.4. Facebook's Racial Discrimination Lawsuit 34
- 11. Riding the Wave: Preparing for an AI-Driven Future in Advertising 35
  - 11.1. Making Sense of the New Normal 35
  - 11.2. Precision Targeting: AI's Secret Sauce 36
  - 11.3. Real-Time Analytics and AI: A Match Made in Heaven 36
  - 11.4. Celebrating the AI Advantage 37
  - 11.5. Building Brands for the AI Future 37
  - 11.6. AI-Powered Reality: A Parting Note 38

Chapter 1. Introduction

As our world becomes ever more digitized, artificial intelligence (AI) is quickly emerging as a key player in the way businesses interact with consumers, especially in the realm of advertising. This Special Report, "AI and the Future of Advertising: Precise Targeting and Real-Time Analytics," delves into the fascinating convergence of cutting-edge technology and marketing strategy. But don't worry, we've tackled the details in a way that is easy to decipher, notwithstanding the technical nature of AI. We study its role in powering precise targeting that can help businesses connect with their ideal audiences and how real-time analytics permits intelligent decision-making to drive sales. So whether you're a tech-savvy insider or just curious about how AI may reshape the advertising landscape, this Special Report is a must-read!

Chapter 2. The Rise of AI in Advertising

The progression of artificial intelligence (AI) has drastically shifted the methods of conducting business operations, particularly in the advertising industry. Significant advancements in AI have equipped the advertising sector to move beyond mere demographics and to aim at targets with pinpoint accuracy. The following discussion elucidates the indispensable role played by AI in advertising.

2.1. The Advent of AI in Advertising

The inception of AI into advertising can be traced back to the rapid digitalization of the economy. Through advancements like predictive analytics and machine learning, companies have successfully utilized AI to process data at an unprecedented speed and scale, creating numerous possibilities in the ad world. Historically, advertisements have been based on demos and psychographics gathered manually. However, AI allows for accurate consumer profiling and prediction of consumer behavior through algorithms, making advertising more relevant and targeted.

2.2. From Traditional Advertising to AI-Infused Strategies

The shift from traditional forms of advertising to sophisticated AI applications has created unprecedented efficiencies in market segmentation, targeting, and positioning. Traditional advertising methods were predominantly scattered and generic, leading to abundant wasted resources in reaching unintended audiences. Proliferation of AI amidst this chaos streamlined the process by employing machine learning algorithms and big data to analyze and predict consumer behavior.

AI in advertising is not restricted merely to consumer identification. It harnesses the power of natural language processing (NLP) to understand the subtleties of human language, allowing advertisers to craft messages that are more personalized and resonate deeply with the targeted audience. AI's capabilities in image, voice, and sentiment recognition have further revolutionized ad personalization, making advertisements more effective and efficient.

2.3. Harnessing Machine Learning for Predictive Analysis

Machine learning (ML), a subtype of AI, has revolutionized the advertising industry with predictive analysis. ML algorithms can analyze complex datasets to predict future actions based on past patterns. For advertisers, this means understanding what will resonate with their target markets before they even initiate campaigns. Furthermore, ML algorithms are continuously learning and refining their predictions, enabling advertisers to optimize their strategies in real-time based upon customer responses.

2.4. AI and Programmatic Advertising

A hallmark application of AI in advertising, programmatic advertising automates the decision-making process of media buying by targeting specific audiences and demographics. Programmatic ads are bought and sold on a per-impression basis, through an auction that happens in real-time. This optimizes the advertisers' budget by ensuring that the ad is only displayed to the desired audience.

AI significantly increases the efficiency and effectiveness of programmatic advertising. Through AI algorithms, these platforms can analyze a visitor's behavior in real-time and decide which ad is most likely to result in a conversion. This technology enables advertisers to dynamically adjust the pricing, placement, and timing of their ads to achieve the highest ROI.

2.5. The Future Of AI In Advertising

The role of AI in advertising is expanding rapidly. With the use of AI-embedded chatbots, companies can generate instant responses to customer inquiries, providing 24/7 customer support. These chatbots can simulate human conversation and handle multiple customer requests concurrently, driving customer engagement and satisfaction while providing immediate and accurate information.

Moreover, AI can analyze and respond to social media trends, helping to shape advertising campaigns in real-time. It can monitor consumer behavior patterns, social interaction, and online activity to predict future behavior and shape ad content, providing companies with an upper hand in crafting their advertising strategies.

In the future, AI is likely to foster an era of hyperpersonalized advertisements. With further advancements, AI algorithms will improve, looking more closely at each individual's unique preferences and tastes, ensuring that advertising content is increasingly relevant and engaging - resulting in improved customer experience and revenue growth.

In summary, AI is revolutionizing the advertising industry and its potential is only just beginning to be realized. From enabling precise targeting to real-time analytics, the rise of AI in advertising offers a plethora of opportunities for companies to optimize their advertising efforts and achieve a higher return on ad spend. As AI continues to evolve and mature, the future of advertising looks smarter, more efficient, and more personal than ever before.

Chapter 3. Understanding the Logic of AI and Machine Learning

Before we delve into the intersection of AI and machine learning with advertising, it's essential to understand the fundamental principles that dictate the operations of these technologies. Knowing how these digital tools work will equip us with the skills to adopt them into our advertising approaches optimally.

3.1. Artificial Intelligence: A Primer

AI is a broad scope of computer science that deals with building smart devices capable of performing tasks that would typically require human intelligence. These tasks might encompass understanding natural language, recognizing patterns, problem-solving, and decision-making.

A rudimentary form of AI can follow explicitly designed algorithms for each task, up to a certain level of complexity. However, traditional algorithm-based approaches reach their limits when the problem domain becomes too large or complex. This is where machine learning comes in.

3.2. The Era of Machine Learning

Machine Learning (ML) is a subset of artificial intelligence. It imparts learning abilities to computers, enabling them to improve from experience and adapt over time. In other words, ML algorithms learn from data, and they become more effective as the volume of data they're exposed to increases.

The central concept in machine learning is the model - a simplified representation of reality that the computer can understand. The machine learning model is generated from the training data, which is a set of samples for which the answer is known. The learning algorithm fine-tunes the parameters of the model based on the input and output of the training data.

These models can be categorized into two main types: supervised learning models and unsupervised learning models.

3.3. Supervised versus Unsupervised Learning Models

1. Supervised Learning: In supervised learning, the training data includes the desired output (label). The machine learning algorithm's goal is to find patterns in the data that correlate the input to the output. Once the patterns are established, the trained model can apply them to new, unseen data, to predict the output.

2. Unsupervised Learning: Unsupervised learning differs as the training data does not include the desired output. The aim here is to discover the inherent structure in the data. Unsupervised learning methods are used for clustering (grouping similar items) and association (discerning rules that describe the data).

3.4. Making Machines Learn: An Overview of ML Process

The machine learning process consists of several stages:

1. Problem understanding and formulation: This involves defining the problem clearly and determining whether machine learning is a feasible solution.

2. Data collection: This involves gathering all the relevant data that

may be needed to solve the problem. It can include data scraping, surveys, or the use of existing databases.

3. Data preparation: This entails cleaning the data and augmenting it if required. It may include removing outliers, dealing with missing data, data normalization.

4. Choosing a suitable model: There are a plethora of machine learning models. The right model is chosen based on the nature of the data and the problem to be solved.

5. Training the model: During this phase, the machine learning algorithm adjusts the model's parameters to minimize the difference between the actual and predicted outputs.

6. Evaluating the model: The model's performance is tested on unseen data to ensure it generalizes well and does not overfit, i.e., it doesn't overly tailor to the training data and performs poorly on new data.

7. Deployment and monitoring: Once satisfied with the model's performance, it's deployed in a real-world system. The model's performance is routinely evaluated to ensure it continues to perform adequately.

In conclusion, AI and machine learning are two critical technologies for developing intelligent systems. By understanding the construct of these systems, one can better appreciate how they can be harnessed effectively for precise targeting in advertising and achieving valuable real-time analytics.

Chapter 4. Unlocking the Potential of Precise Targeting

AI has given marketers an unprecedented level of specificity to not just target a generalized demographic, but to also individualize the targeting based on nuanced, personal information. The implications of this technology are broad, but one key takeaway is the ability for marketers to improve the efficiency and efficacy of their campaigns.

4.1. Defining Precise Targeting

Precise targeting, often also referred to as narrowcasting, micro-targeting or hyper-targeting, is the process of sending personalized messages or content to a specific, segmented and nuanced group of customers. It's a direct response to mass marketing practices that cast a wide net but rarely get to the heart of what individual consumers want or need. AI excels at both identifying these groups and crafting precise targeting campaigns around them.

Broadly, precise targeting can be seen as an umbrella term for utilizing data to deliver customized advertising content. However, in the era of AI, precise targeting has become far more sophisticated by applying machine learning algorithms and data analysis to target specific consumer groups based on behavior, interest, demographics and location.

4.2. The Role of AI in Precise Targeting

Artificial Intelligence (AI) brings a heightened level of sophistication to precise targeting. AI algorithms can analyze large amounts of data quickly, recognizing patterns and preferences that humans might overlook. Once these patterns are understood, AI can segment and target groups or individuals at an unprecedented granularity.

One key element of AI's role in precise targeting is its ability to analyze and process vast quantities of data. Every interaction a consumer has online provides a piece of data. This data is often unstructured and vast, creating a challenge for traditional data analysis methods.

However, AI can harness this data and extract meaningful insights from it. Machine learning algorithms can spot trends and predict future behavior by analyzing past behaviors. Neural networks can take in massive amounts of data points, identify correlations and create consumer profiles accordingly.

4.3. Real-World Applications

But how does precise targeting facilitated by AI look in practice? Let's explore some real-world examples of AI's impressive capability:

1. Social Media Advertising: AI is the engine that powers the highly targeted ads that you see on social media platforms. It uses the data provided by users (both proactive and derived) to create detailed profiles, allowing advertisers to target a specific age group, in a specific location, with specific interests.

2. Programmatic Advertising: Programmatic advertising refers to the use of AI to buy and sell online advertising space in real time. This method incorporates vast amounts of data, deciding in milliseconds who the ad will be shown to based on market segmentation and behavior prediction models.

3. Personalized E-commerce Experiences: E-commerce sites use AI to provide personalized product recommendations. These recommendations are curated based on data regarding browsing and purchasing history. This is precise targeting on a micro level as it's individually based.

4.4. Harnessing the Right Data

For precise targeting to be truly effective, marketers need to harness the right kind of data. Broadly, the data utilized for precise targeting can be categorized into three types:

1. **Demographic Data**: This includes age, gender, income, occupation, and more.
2. **Behavioral Data**: This encompasses online habits, preferred channels of interaction, buying preferences, and more.
3. **Psychographic Data**: This includes a customer's values, attitudes, opinions, interests, and lifestyle.

AI-powered tools streamline the process of gathering, storing, and analyzing this data. With machine learning, the collection and interpretation of this data become automated, making the process more time and cost-efficient.

4.5. Leaps and Bounds: The Future of Precise Targeting

The future of precise targeting is exciting, with potential advancements in AI promising even more granularity. While the current state of AI can tag attributes and classify them (i.e. recognize an individual's gender, age, location), the next step would see AI deciphering context and emotions to target consumers at an even deeper, more personalized level. Advancements in AI technology like emotional AI or NLP (Natural Language Processing) will provide the ability to understand user sentiments based on their online activity and tailor advertisements accordingly.

Finally, the marriage of AI and precise targeting has benefits for both marketers and consumers. For marketers, it presents opportunities to create highly targeted campaigns that yield higher conversions and engagement. For consumers, it means less irrelevant ads and more content that resonates with their needs, interests and lifestyles. The ability to engage consumers with personalized advertising can create longer-lasting relationships between a brand and its audience.

In conclusion, AI enhanced precise targeting is not a distant reality, but the modus operandi of today. As AI capabilities continue to unfold, anticipate further reshaping of the marketing and advertising digital landscape with precision and personalization at its core.

Chapter 5. Exploring Real-Time Analytics and its Impact

In an era where businesses constantly seek innovative ways to make data-driven decisions, real-time analytics powered by AI tools have taken center stage. Coupling leading-edge technology with an intuitive understanding of the market, real-time analytics can process vast quantities of data at unprecedented speeds, delivering actionable insights that can help organizations identify customer behaviors, optimize their advertising efforts, and stay steps ahead of the competition.

5.1. Understanding Real-Time Analytics

Real-time analytics refers to the process of analyzing data as soon as it enters the system, offering organizations immediate insights. This functionality is a significant departure from traditional analytics approaches that necessitate collection, storage, and analysis - a process that could take days, weeks, or even months. Real-time analytics' strength lies in speed, providing the potential to transform raw data into valuable action points almost instantaneously.

The foundation of real-time analytics is 'stream processing.' This technique is capable of analyzing and taking action on real-time data. AI plays a crucial role in this process, utilizing machine learning algorithms to identify patterns and make predictive analytics more accurate.

5.2. The Intersection of AI and Real-time Analytics

AI algorithms are designed to learn from data and make decisions or predictions based on their learning. In the context of real-time analytics, AI can make exceptionally quick decisions based on the latest data, adjusting advertising strategies to maximize opportunities or limit potential problems. Machine Learning (ML), a subset of AI, can process big data analytics to predict user behaviors based on their past actions.

Advancements in technology have now made it possible to analyze not only structured data like demographics and purchase history but also unstructured data, such as social media posts, images, or natural language. This holistic approach provides a 360-degree view of consumers, which, when combined with real-time data, enables even more precise advertising targeting.

5.3. Impact of Real-Time Analytics on Advertising

We now turn our attention to the various ways real-time analytics drives change in the advertising industry.

1. **Personalization and Precision Targeting:** With real-time analytics, businesses can capture and capitalize on an individual's 'digital moments,' or interactions with the brand. Based on behaviors such as browsing history, purchase actions, and social media activities, AI can tailor unique advertisements suiting each user. Personalization can boost conversion rates and enhance customer loyalty.
2. **Real-Time Bidding:** Real-time analytics make real-time bidding (RTB) possible. RTB involves the buying and selling of ad

impressions in real time, where the highest bidder wins the chance to display their ad to a potential customer. RTB depends on immediate analysis of user data to make quick, informed decisions.

3. **Predictive Analysis for Ad Optimization:** By analyzing real-time data, AI can predict the most effective ad timing, format, and content. Predictive analysis helps advertisers optimize their campaigns and maximize their Return On Investment (ROI).

4. **Fraud Detection:** Real-time analytics can spot unusual patterns that may indicate fraudulent activity, helping businesses act quickly to prevent damage.

5.4. Challenges in Implementation

While the benefits of real-time analytics are evident, several challenges remain for its full-scale implementation.

1. **Data Quality and Integrity:** Ensuring the accuracy and consistency of real-time data can be demanding, with the risk of compromised data leading to inaccurate results and poor decision-making.

2. **Infrastructure Requirements:** The infrastructure capable of supporting real-time analytics can be costly to implement and maintain.

3. **Privacy Concerns:** As businesses analyze more data in real time, considerations around consumer privacy and data protection become even more critical, with strict legal requirements in this arena.

Despite these challenges, the potential of AI and real-time analytics in advertising cannot be understated. As technologies continue to progress and advance, we can expect a future where advertising success leans more heavily on the direct, actionable insights delivered by real-time analytics. The real-time nature of this innovative technology means organizations can adjust their strategies on the fly, making advertising more adaptable, personalized, and responsive than ever before. As we continue into an increasingly data-driven age, adopting a real-time analytics approach in advertising will not merely be an option; it will be a necessity.

Chapter 6. Cracking the Code: How Algorithms Shape Ads

As we embark on our digital journey, algorithms stand as the computational powerhouses defining the direction of online advertising. They are the driver that shapes our digital footprint and influences the content that we interact with. Delving into these behind-the-scenes players surfaces the vast sophistication and influence they harbor in the realm of advertising.

6.1. The Basics of Algorithms

When you hear the term algorithm, it denotes a step-by-step procedure at its heart, which is crafted to perform specific tasks. In the realm of digital advertising, these tasks could range from deciding which audience to target, what time to display an ad, or determining the effectiveness of an advertising campaign. All these decisions are derived from analyzing loads of data that we generate as we navigate the digital space.

An algorithm analyzes this data, learns patterns and makes predictions. It uses a variety of techniques from across computer science, mathematics, and statistics to achieve this. Though it might seem like an ethereal, abstract concept, an algorithm is rather concrete and has an intrinsic method at its core. It tries to achieve an output from an input using methodical and logical steps.

Let's take an example of a simple advertising algorithm. Whenever you search for a particular product on an e-commerce site, the algorithm studies that search and uses it to recommend other similar products to the user. This recommendation algorithm is powered by principles such as collaborative filtering, which matches users based on their search histories, and content-based systems, which match users with content based on the description of the products they have viewed or purchased in the past.

6.2. Advanced Algorithmic Techniques

While the above example is rather simple, modern advertising algorithms used by major online platforms are incredibly sophisticated. They harness advanced techniques like machine learning (ML) and artificial intelligence to analyze high-dimensional, large-scale data, making incredibly quick and precise decisions.

Machine Learning, a subset of artificial intelligence, refers to statistical models that learn from data and subsequently make predictions. In advertising, machine learning algorithms learn from past user behavior trends and make predictions about future behavior.

For instance, if a user often clicks on ads for skincare products, a machine learning algorithm will learn this pattern and begin showing this user more skincare-related ads. It continues to learn and refine its predictions over time, adjusting to user's ever-evolving tastes, ensuring that the ads displayed are always relevant.

6.3. Real-life Applications of Algorithms

Algorithms, particularly those employed by Google and Facebook, have defined the current era of digital advertising. They operate on massive troves of data, processing billions of user interactions to serve targeted ads that align with individual behaviors, preferences, and inclinations.

On Facebook, the ad auction algorithm determines which ads to show to which users based on dozens of factors, including the relevancy score of the ad, the bid placed by the advertiser, and the estimated action rates (which predict the likelihood of the user taking the advertiser's desired action). Similarly, Google's Ad Rank algorithm determines where an ad gets placed in search results based on the quality score and the bid amount.

For both these platforms, a substantial part of the algorithm's utility is also directed towards maintaining user experience. They work meticulously to prevent ad fatigue - the scenario where a user sees the same ad too many times - and ensure that the advertising content a consumer sees is relevant and valuable to them.

6.4. Algorithms as Agents of Precision

The level of precision targeted advertising achieved by algorithms allows businesses to reach their ideal audiences, ensuring a higher return on investment for their marketing efforts. By using data about consumers' online behaviors, algorithms help companies display their ads to those consumers most likely to be interested in their products or services.

This precision is not only useful for large corporations. Small businesses also benefit immensely, as they can direct their often-limited advertising budgets to the specific audiences that they are most likely to succeed with. In essence, algorithms have democratized the playing field, offering precision-targeted advertising capabilities to businesses of all sizes.

6.5. The Future of Advertising Algorithms

The role and importance of algorithms are poised to amplify in the future. With the arrival of 5G and the predicted explosion in datapoints from the Internet of things (IoT), advertising algorithms will have much more data to work with. This will result in ads that are even more customizable and optimized.

However, with increasing algorithmic sophistication also comes greater responsibility. Issues of data privacy, algorithmic transparency, and digital equity need to be given paramount importance. As law and society evolve to address these concerns, it's crucial that the use of algorithms aligns with a future that values not just economic efficiency but ethical fairness.

In conclusion, the currents of advertising are being influenced more and more by the AI-powered sails of algorithms. Looking forward, as algorithms continue to shape and drive the advertising industry, keeping yourself informed and abreast of such changes is undoubtedly a wise choice.

Chapter 7. Personalization and Predictive Analysis: The Future

The continuous evolution of technology is causing seismic shifts in marketing and advertising. Central to this transformational revolution is the intersection of Artificial Intelligence (AI) and Big Data. Two concepts that spring from this union are personalization and predictive analysis. These advancements have given rise to novel ways of optimizing the marketing funnel, leading to more personal, precise, and timely communication between businesses and prospective customers, increasing both engagement and conversion rates.

7.1. Role of AI in Personalization

In the world of advertising, AI has become a potent tool for personalization — tailoring content, communications, and user experiences to individual users. This personalization results in a significant rise in customer satisfaction, brand loyalty, and ultimately, revenue.

AI processes vast quantities of data — including user-profile information, browsing histories, and behavioral data — to understand individual consumer preferences, translate them into actionable insights, and automate personalized content delivery. Collaborative filtering, for example, is an AI-driven recommendation algorithm widely used by e-commerce platforms such as Amazon and Netflix for personalized product suggestions. Such suggestions are derived from an individual user's history, as well as the behaviors of similar users.

Another example is content personalization, where AI-powered tools create tailored digital experiences. These experiences are in the form of personalized emails, customized website content, or targeted offers, which give the feeling of a one-on-one interaction between the brand and the consumer.

7.2. Importance of Predictive Analysis

Alongside personalization, predictive analysis has also come to the fore, thanks to advancements in machine learning, a subfield of AI. Predictive analysis uses historical data, statistical algorithms, and machine learning techniques to identify potential future outcomes based on past data.

In the context of advertising, predictive analysis can forecast customer behaviors, purchase patterns, and market trends. For instance, predictive models can identify potential churn risks, enabling businesses to take proactive measures to retain customers. Predictive analytics can also anticipate future sales trends, ensuring that companies are well-prepared to meet demand.

Predictive analytics further helps in optimizing ad spend. By predicting which marketing channels are likely to yield the best results, businesses can allocate resources efficiently, maximizing return on investment (ROI).

7.3. Combining Personalization with Predictive Analysis

Bringing together the capabilities of personalization and predictive analysis allows marketers to deliver hyper-relevant messages to consumers at the exact right moment — a game-changing tactic known as predictive personalization.

Through predictive personalization, AI-powered platforms can anticipate a consumer's next move before they make it, and then quickly act on that insight to deliver relevant content. This ability to predict and act in real time creates a more dynamic user experience that encourages engagement and conversion.

7.4. Real-Life Applications and Case Studies

Let's take the example of streaming giant Netflix. AI sits firmly at the helm of Netflix's personalization strategy. From recommending what shows users should watch next to deciding the artwork each user sees for a particular show, everything is in line with the individual user's preferences.

On the other hand, predictive analytics allows Netflix to predict possible churn, subscriber viewing preferences, and most importantly, the potential success of new shows, helping them invest wisely.

Google Adwords, too, uses predictive analytics to forecast the success of marketing campaigns. Their 'Smart Bidding' system uses machine learning to automatically optimize bids for conversions or conversion value in each auction—a feature known as 'auction-time bidding.'

Fashion retailer, Stitch Fix, combines personalization and predictive analysis to create a unique business model. Their AI-driven platform asks users about their style preferences, sizes, and price points, among other things. This data is then used to personalize the style recommendations, while predictive analysis is used to forecast trends and manage inventory.

7.5. The Road Ahead: Challenges and Opportunities

As fantastical as the merger of AI-driven personalization and predictive analytics may sound, it isn't without its challenges. Key among these are concerns related to data privacy and the ethics of data manipulation, algorithmic bias, and the need for massive computational power.

Yet, the opportunities far outweigh these challenges. As technology advances, personalization and predictive analysis will likely become even more refined, resulting in an unprecedented level of accuracy in targeted advertising.

Employing AI's capabilities can unlock new levels of growth and success for businesses, offering a blend of personalization and predictability that was previously unthinkable. Thus, it goes without saying that mastering personalization and predictive analysis is crucial to future-proofing any advertising strategy.

In conclusion, the future of advertising lies in the harmonious blend of personalization and predictive analysis powered by AI. As we brace for the fantastic ride ahead, we can be assured that the days of spray and pray advertising are long behind us. The future is here, and it's personal, predictive, and phenomenally precise.

Chapter 8. The Ethical Considerations in AI Advertising

Advertising is not just about selling products or services - it's about communication with potential customers, allowing businesses to display their unique selling propositions to a potentially receptive audience. The advent of AI in advertising has entirely transformed this landscape, promising unprecedented efficiency in terms of targeted ad placements and real-time analytics. However, while contemplating the potential merits of AI-driven advertising, it's also crucial to reflect on the ethical implications, including issues related to privacy, discrimination, transparency, and more.

8.1. Privacy Concerns

Cutting-edge AI algorithms used in advertising often rely heavily on data about users' online behavior, shopping habits, and personal preferences. While this allows companies to tailor messages towards specific audiences, it raises serious concerns about privacy. How much data is appropriate to collect, and how should it be used?

AI applications like machine learning and predictive analysis permit highly granular profiling of individuals. A user's digital footprint, combined with additional information from various sources, can paint a detailed picture of their interests, tendencies, preferences, and even weaknesses. The utilization of personal data can leave people feeling watched, tracked, and exploited, with their privacy fundamentally invaded.

Moreover, in certain scenarios, the data leveraged by AI algorithms may include sensitive information such as an individual's health status, financial situation, or political views. Unauthorized or inadvertent disclosure of such information, whether it happens through data breaches or other scenarios, can yield severe harmful consequences.

Organizations using AI in their advertising must therefore prioritize privacy and security. Businesses must strive to strike a balance, using data to inform decisions but also respecting consumers' rights to privacy. Transparency about data collection practices, security measures to safeguard information and appropriate limits regarding how long and for what purpose data is stored should be standard.

8.2. Algorithmic Bias and Discrimination

AI algorithms are not born bias-free. Instead, they inherit their biases from the training data used to teach them. If this underlying data is skewed or unrepresentative, the AI software may unintentionally perpetuate existing societal biases by excluding or discriminating against particular groups.

For example, an advertisement algorithm trained solely on data from wealthier users might unfairly marginalize lower-income groups. It might choose to display expensive luxury product ads to wealthy customers while excluding lower-income consumers, thus reinforcing economic inequality.

Likewise, biased algorithms might promote harmful stereotypes, for instance, by presenting certain jobs or products as gender-specific, even though they're not. Companies need to be aware of these risks and take credible steps to ensure that their AI-powered marketing activities do not inadvertently promote discrimination or exclusion.

8.3. Transparency and Explainability

AI-powered advertising can be incredibly complex, leading to situations where even those behind the algorithms do not completely understand the patterns and correlations being used to target ads. This lack of transparency and explainability, known as the 'black box' problem, is another crucial ethical issue.

Consumers have a right to understand how their personal data influences the advertisements they receive. For example, if someone is consistently shown ads for a specific product or service, they may wish to know why.

In the quest to make targeted advertising more transparent, business models could incorporate methods to inform consumers why they are targeted for specific ads based on data or AI-driven decisions. However, this needs to be done in a manner that respects consumer understanding, fearing not to overload the consumer with complex AI mechanics, but rather to present just enough detail for informed consent.

8.4. The Monopoly Problem

AI algorithms, especially in digital advertising, tend to favor major players or market leaders. Smaller businesses or new entrants might suffer, struggling to make their voice heard in a system that inherently prefers larger companies with more resources and data at their disposal. This could eventually lead to a monopolistic market scenario, where only a handful of large entities influence customer choices and determine market trends, stifering market competition.

Organizations need to engage in fair trade practice, ensuring that their AI algorithms are not being exploited to suppress competition. Regulatory bodies need to enforce laws and ensure the market remains conducive to competition, enabling every player, regardless of their size, to reach out to their potential audience.

AI is poised to change the face of advertising, offering unparalleled insights and capabilities for targeted marketing. However, it's clear that ethical considerations, including privacy, discrimination, transparency, and the risk of monopolization, are clear challenges that need to be addressed. As AI continues to be integrated and developed, it is essential for businesses to act responsibly, considering not just what AI can do, but also what it should do.

Chapter 9. Interpreting Big Data in Ads and Marketing

Artificial Intelligence (AI) is revolutionizing various sectors in unprecedented ways, and advertising is no exception. In this era of intense competition, it's vital for businesses to streamline their marketing efforts and harness the potential of big data to identify trends, understand customer behaviors, and align their strategies accordingly.

9.1. The Role of Big Data in Advertising

Big data, in the context of advertising, is a vast and diverse collection of information used to understand individual and group behaviors, interests, and patterns. It comprises raw, semi-structured, and structured data collected and processed from myriad sources such as social media, websites, mobile apps, IoT devices, CRMs, and market research.

Big data in advertising fuels precise targeting, customer segmentation, and personalized ad content. A profound understanding of each customer's unique desires, needs, and behaviors, powered by big data analytics, leads to more customer engagement and ultimately, higher conversion rates.

===Data Collection and Management: Foundation of Big Data in Advertising

Collecting and managing high-volume data is a formidable task. It requires effective and efficient mechanisms to handle the vast amount and variety of data, ensuring data accuracy, relevancy, and timeliness.

AI-powered tools aid in managing the data collection process, from data aggregation, cleaning, validation, storage to assessment. Data management platforms (DMPs) collect data from both first-party and third-party sources, classify the data based on attributes such as demographics, behaviors, and interests and store it in an organized, accessible manner. AI models can refine these processes, offering better data aggregation and classification, leading to a more robust data foundation for subsequent analyses.

9.2. Big Data Analytics: Transforming Raw Data into Insights

Once big data is collected, the next crucial task is to analyze the data and transform it into meaningful insights. Big data analytics is a suite of data analysis methods applied to large data sets that extract actionable information.

AI steps in here, solving possibly the most significant big data challenge - the sheer volume makes manual analysis impossible and conventional processing applications inadequate. With machine learning algorithms, AI can sift through vast amounts of data, identify patterns, decode trends, and predict future consumer behavior.

AI-based tools such as predictive algorithms and data mining techniques have become indispensable in modern advertising campaigns. These tools analyze past customer data to predict future behavior, guide advertisers on when and where to place their ads, and define ad content that would resonate most with a certain audience group.

===Personalization and Targeted Advertising: The Power of Big Data

Personalization is a key marketing strategy that necessitates the accurate targeting of customers. Big data's ability to provide detailed insights into consumer habits and preferences enables this precision.

AI-powered analysis can segment consumers into different groups based on demographics, purchasing behaviors, and personal interests, among other attributes. Each segment can then receive personalized messages, ensuring relevance and increasing the likelihood of conversion.

This level of personalization becomes especially powerful in online advertising. Here, big data analytics can use real-time browsing data to serve personalized ads in milliseconds. For instance, retargeting - showing products that the consumer has shown interest in but not yet purchased - is an effective strategy enabled by big data.

9.3. Real-time Analytics: Enabling Dynamic Marketing Strategies

Big data is not only about volume but also about speed. Leveraging real-time analytics helps businesses adjust their strategies on the fly, based on the latest customer interactions.

AI-powered real-time analytics provide businesses with an accurate and up-to-date view of how their ads are performing. Real-time data can inform ad placement, content, and pricing decisions dynamically as market conditions, consumer preferences, or competition shift.

Such real-time, data-driven strategies give businesses an edge in the ever-evolving digital advertising landscape.

In conclusion, the intersection of big data and AI is set to revolutionize the advertising industry, reshaping how businesses strategize, execute, and measure the effectiveness of their campaigns. As these technologies continue to evolve and mature, the advertising techniques made possible will become more refined, offering businesses more opportunities to connect meaningfully with their audiences.

Chapter 10. Case Studies: Successes and Failures in AI Advertising

The path of AI in advertising has not always been smooth, with both remarkable successes and notable failures shaping its trajectory.

10.1. The Netflix Algorithm: A Growth Engine

One of the most extraordinary examples of AI in advertising is its application by Netflix. With over 200 million subscribers, Netflix has a voluminous vault of consumer watching habits, preferences, and behaviors. They have developed an AI algorithm that regularly sifts through this data, providing customized, relevant recommendations to each user. This personalized attention is translated into advertisements as viewers are marketed new shows or movies they are most likely to watch and enjoy.

Netflix no longer pushes blanket promotions for its latest releases to all its subscribers. Instead, it has mastered the art of segmentation and targeting by leveraging its algorithm. It has made Netflix more engaging and user-friendly, converting single-time watchers into loyal subscribers. This advanced, customized advertising has driven the company's growth and ensured customer retention.

However, the algorithm's potential doesn't stop at recommendations. Netflix uses it to strategically decide which shows to finance or purchase. It merges viewing habits, general popularity, and anticipated trends to predict the success probabilities of prospective content. AI becomes instrumental in strategic decision-making, which directly, though indirectly, impacts advertising.

10.2. Unilever: Improving Efficiency and Accuracy

Unilever, a consumer goods company with diverse products, encountered a growing issue in managing its complex product portfolio effectively. It turned to AI to improve the efficiency and accuracy of their advertising strategy.

Unilever leveraged AI algorithms to analyze its extensive consumer data and recognize patterns in purchasing behavior. The AI insights allowed for precise targeting and detailed customer profiling. The intelligent system also used real-time analytics to identify the most effective marketing channels, ideal ad timing, and preferential content for different consumer segments.

The results were remarkable. Unilever saw a significant increase in engagement, translating into increased sales and market share. There was an undeniable scale of optimization that could have only been achieved by leveraging AI, a surefire success in the realm of precision advertising.

10.3. The Google Flu Trends Flop

Not all AI projects meet with success—sometimes, they experience catastrophic failures. A classic example is Google Flu Trends. An AI model was set up to predict where flu outbreaks would occur, based on patterns in search terms related to flu symptoms. The idea was promising, but faced an unfortunate reality when the AI failed to predict the flu epidemic of 2013 correctly.

Due to unforeseen consumer behavior and the model's inability to adjust to it, the AI system overestimated the impact by approximately twice the actual flu cases. The system was too heavily dependent on user-generated data without considering external influences like media panic or hype. Moreover, the failure pointed out the larger issue, the AI model's inability to understand the nuances and everchanging nature of human behavior.

Its downfall served as an invaluable lesson about the limitations of AI—even with perceivable patterns, there exist inherent, unpredictable variations in human behavior which AI may not feasibly anticipate.

10.4. Facebook's Racial Discrimination Lawsuit

Sometimes friction with AI technology can occur due to ethical issues. Facebook, amidst all its AI-driven advertising success, ended up in a complicated lawsuit in 2019. Facebook's AI had enabled advertisers to target users by age, gender, and, controversially, race. The real estate industry took advantage of these AI capabilities to restrict housing-related ads from some racial groups.

This act of precision targeting went too far, igniting the debate on "micro-targeting" and whether there should be ethical constraints to AI's capabilities. It highlighted a significant risk of AI technology – there must be guidelines and meaningful restrictions to avoid misuse.

In conclusion, the adoption of AI in advertising ventures often turns into a double-edged sword immensely beneficial when executed correctly, but equally destructive when it fails. To ensure success, companies need to understand the capability of their AI systems fully, set meaningful boundaries and remain adaptable to the unpredictable nature of consumer behavior. Without these cautionary measures, they might run the risk of outsmarting themselves through their use of AI. Understanding these case studies offers a guide to the intricate relationship between AI and future advertising.

Chapter 11. Riding the Wave: Preparing for an AI-Driven Future in Advertising

The widespread emergence and rise of artificial intelligence has resulted in an impromptu shake-up in the mechanism by which many business sectors operate. The realm of advertising is not exempt from this disruptive dynamic. As traditional advertising methods become increasingly ineffective and obsolete, marketers are compelled to navigate and ride this wave of artificial intelligence that has the potential to revolutionize the advertising landscape.

11.1. Making Sense of the New Normal

AI's evolution in recent years has profoundly altered consumer expectations as well as the strategies businesses employ to engage, capture, and maintain customer attention. Consumers now demand curated, personalized experiences tailored to specific needs, preferences, and behaviors. Furthermore, the drive for digital transformation has necessitated a shift towards data-driven decision-making, with an emphasis on real-time insights and dynamic customization.

In this interaction, AI holds tremendous promise. It serves as the catalyst for precision-targeted campaigns that reach potential customers in their preferred mediums, at the right time, and in a context that resonates with them. It further enables real-time analytics to monitor performance, customize strategies instantly, and ensure sustained engagement and conversion.

11.2. Precision Targeting: AI's Secret Sauce

AI's core strength lies in its capacity to analyze vast quantities of complex, unstructured data swiftly and accurately. The use of AI in advertising notably simplifies a common issue faced by advertisers: reaching out to the right audience at the right time with the right message. By implementing AI algorithms, marketers can accurately track and predict consumer behaviors.

Machine learning, a subset of AI, helps in identifying patterns within large data sets to recognize common grouping factors, likely triggers for actions, and indicators of a specific need or interest. As such, machine learning facilitates the creation of consumer clusters or personas, which can then be targeted with aptly customized content. This precise targeting results in higher conversion rates, since the ad's message is tailored to the recipient's profile and their current position in the purchase journey.

11.3. Real-Time Analytics and AI: A Match Made in Heaven

AI isn't just about hitting the perfect target; it's also about refining and optimizing advertising tactics in real-time using ever-evolving data analytics. AI-based systems make use of predictive analytics and data mining to create dynamic consumer profiles that modify and adjust according to new data.

The brilliance of real-time analytics rests on its capacity to capture and report on the behavioral data immediately after an event has occurred. From the moment a user clicks on an advert to their journey on the website, real-time analytics allow every action to be tracked, analyzed, and acted upon promptly.

Such analytics can be harnessed to adjust and improve marketing strategies instantly, ensuring that the ad content, target demographic, and even the medium are most effective. Data points can be plugged back into the machine learning algorithm to continually refine and improve the precision of targeting, thus creating a virtuous cycle of improvement and refinement.

11.4. Celebrating the AI Advantage

Another significant stride that AI brings to the table is the capacity for brands and advertisers to maintain continuity and consistency across various platforms. From social media, websites, and email to more conventional media such as television and press, an AI-enabled system can ensure automated consistency. By aggregating data across platforms in real-time, AI can reduce data silos, improve information consistency, optimize user experience, and ultimately boost conversion rates.

11.5. Building Brands for the AI Future

Adopting AI is not merely about leveraging technology; rather, it is about refashioning the organizational mindset to align with the fast-paced, AI-driven world. It is about creating a corporate culture that recognizes the value of data, nurtures innovation, and is agile enough to adjust to shifting customer expectations and behaviors.

There is a need for organizations to invest in knowledge capital, technical infrastructure, and partnerships to effectively harness the potential of AI in advertising. This includes recruiting and training data scientists, investing in data management platforms, and choosing partners with AI capabilities.

11.6. AI-Powered Reality: A Parting Note

As we transition into a more AI-driven advertising landscape, the radical changes will necessitate a substantial shift in thought processes, strategies, and organizational structures. However, as daunting as the ride may initially appear, the rewards in terms of precision targeting, real-time analytics, and improved customer engagement make AI an irresistible change agent.

Artificial Intelligence brings a previously unparalleled level of personalization and precision in the competitive industry of advertising. It signifies a substantial shift from a broad, generic customer chase towards a more nuanced, targeted, and efficient approach. However, the ride promises to be as rewarding as it is challenging. Businesses ready to adapt, learn, and embrace AI will gear up to ride the wave and emerge successfully in this future of advertising.

Finally, it is important to remember that while AI can provide powerful tools and insights, it cannot replace the need for robust business strategies and creative approaches. Rather, it can augment and enhance these strategies, leading to transformative impacts. As such, even in an AI-driven future, the human element in advertising and marketing will continue to be vital.

Printed in Great Britain
by Amazon